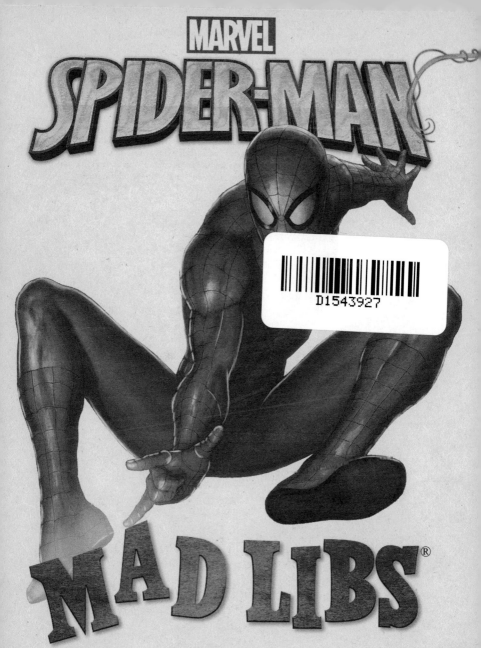

MARVEL

SPIDER-MAN

MAD LIBS®

by Brandon T. Snider

Mad Libs
An Imprint of Penguin Random House

MAD LIBS
Penguin Young Readers Group
An Imprint of Penguin Random House LLC

Mad Libs format copyright © 2017 by Penguin Random House LLC. All rights reserved.

Concept created by Roger Price & Leonard Stern.

© 2017 MARVEL

Published by Mad Libs,
an imprint of Penguin Random House LLC,
345 Hudson Street, New York, New York 10014.
Printed in the USA.

ISBN 9780515157369
3 5 7 9 10 8 6 4

MAD LIBS

INSTRUCTIONS

MAD LIBS® is a game for people who don't like games! It can be played by one, two, three, four, or forty.

• RIDICULOUSLY SIMPLE DIRECTIONS

In this tablet you will find stories containing blank spaces where words are left out. One player, the READER, selects one of these stories. The READER does not tell anyone what the story is about. Instead, he/she asks the other players, the WRITERS, to give him/her words. These words are used to fill in the blank spaces in the story.

• TO PLAY

The READER asks each WRITER in turn to call out a word—an adjective or a noun or whatever the space calls for—and uses them to fill in the blank spaces in the story. The result is a MAD LIBS® game.

When the READER then reads the completed MAD LIBS® game to the other players, they will discover that they have written a story that is fantastic, screamingly funny, shocking, silly, crazy, or just plain dumb—depending upon which words each WRITER called out.

• EXAMPLE (*Before* and *After*)

" _____ !" he said _____
           EXCLAMATION   ADVERB

as he jumped into his convertible _____ and
                                              NOUN

drove off with his _____ wife.
                        ADJECTIVE

" _____OUCH_____ !" he said _____STUPIDLY_____
           EXCLAMATION   ADVERB

as he jumped into his convertible _____CAT_____ and
                                              NOUN

drove off with his _____BRAVE_____ wife.
                        ADJECTIVE

In case you have forgotten what adjectives, adverbs, nouns, and verbs are, here is a quick review:

An ADJECTIVE describes something or somebody. *Lumpy, soft, ugly, messy,* and *short* are adjectives.

An ADVERB tells how something is done. It modifies a verb and usually ends in "ly." *Modestly, stupidly, greedily,* and *carefully* are adverbs.

A NOUN is the name of a person, place, or thing. *Sidewalk, umbrella, bridle, bathtub,* and *nose* are nouns.

A VERB is an action word. *Run, pitch, jump,* and *swim* are verbs. Put the verbs in past tense if the directions say PAST TENSE. *Ran, pitched, jumped,* and *swam* are verbs in the past tense.

When we ask for A PLACE, we mean any sort of place: a country or city (*Spain, Cleveland*) or a room (*bathroom, kitchen*).

An EXCLAMATION or SILLY WORD is any sort of funny sound, gasp, grunt, or outcry, like *Wow!, Ouch!, Whomp!, Ick!,* and *Gadzooks!*

When we ask for specific words, like a NUMBER, a COLOR, an ANIMAL, or a PART OF THE BODY, we mean a word that is one of those things, like *seven, blue, horse,* or *head.*

When we ask for a PLURAL, it means more than one. For example, *cat* pluralized is *cats.*

MAD LIBS® is fun to play with friends, but you can also play it by yourself! To begin with, DO NOT look at the story on the page below. Fill in the blanks on this page with the words called for. Then, using the words you have selected, fill in the blank spaces in the story.

Now you've created your own hilarious MAD LIBS® game!

THE ORIGIN OF SPIDER-MAN

ADJECTIVE _____

A PLACE _____

ANIMAL _____

A PLACE _____

NOUN _____

ADJECTIVE _____

VERB _____

PART OF THE BODY _____

VERB _____

PLURAL NOUN _____

NOUN _____

ADJECTIVE _____

PLURAL NOUN _____

A PLACE _____

NOUN _____

VERB ENDING IN "ING" _____

My name is Peter Parker. You might look at me and think, "He's just

some _____ kid from (the) _____, New York!" but I
　　　　 ADJECTIVE　　　　　　　　　　　　 A PLACE

became a lot more than that the day I was bitten by a radioactive

_____. I was on a class trip to (the) _____ at the
　 ANIMAL　　　　　　　　　　　　　　　　　　　　 A PLACE

time. I am a/an _____ guy, after all. Things got really
　　　　　　　　　　　 NOUN

_____ when I started to _____ weird spider powers.
　 ADJECTIVE　　　　　　　　　　　　 VERB

I thought I was losing my _____! At first I thought I could
　　　　　　　　　　　　　　 PART OF THE BODY

_____ my powers to make some quick _____, but
　 VERB　　　　　　　　　　　　　　　　　　　　　 PLURAL NOUN

then I found myself in real trouble. I failed to stop a/an _____
　　　　　　　　　　　　　　　　　　　　　　　　　　　 NOUN

and lost my _____ Uncle Ben in the process. That's when I
　　　　　　 ADJECTIVE

vowed to use my _____ to help the people of (the)
　　　　　　　　　　 PLURAL NOUN

_____. I made a snazzy _____ and began
　 A PLACE　　　　　　　　　　　　　　 NOUN

_____ around town as the Amazing Spider-Man!
 VERB ENDING IN "ING"

MAD LIBS® is fun to play with friends, but you can also play it by yourself! To begin with, DO NOT look at the story on the page below. Fill in the blanks on this page with the words called for. Then, using the words you have selected, fill in the blank spaces in the story.

Now you've created your own hilarious MAD LIBS® game!

WELCOME TO NEW YORK CITY

NOUN _____

VERB _____

PLURAL NOUN _____

ADJECTIVE _____

VERB ENDING IN "ING" _____

VERB ENDING IN "ING" _____

NOUN _____

COLOR _____

OCCUPATION _____

A PLACE _____

ADJECTIVE _____

ADJECTIVE _____

PLURAL NOUN _____

NOUN _____

ADJECTIVE _____

MAD LIBS
WELCOME TO
NEW YORK CITY

Welcome to New York City or, as locals call it, the _____ that

NOUN

loves to _____! The city is home to many famous

VERB

_____, as well as one of the most _____ heroes of

PLURAL NOUN _____ _ADJECTIVE_

all time: Spider-Man. On any given day you may see him

_____ across town or _____ an evil

VERB ENDING IN "ING" _____ _VERB ENDING IN "ING"_

villain in the middle of Times Square. Don't be afraid. He does that all

the time. During your stay, why not visit the _____ of Liberty?

NOUN

It's that big _____ thing you might have seen on TV. It was a

COLOR

gift from the _____ of (the) _____. Spider-Man

OCCUPATION _____ _A PLACE_

fights bad guys there, too. Oh, and don't forget to check out the

_____ Daily Bugle Building! If you're _____, you

ADJECTIVE _____ _ADJECTIVE_

can catch Spider-Man fighting bad _____ on the building's

PLURAL NOUN

scenic _____. Isn't this city the most _____ place in

NOUN _____ _ADJECTIVE_

the world?

From MARVEL'S SPIDER-MAN MAD LIBS® • Copyright © 2017 MARVEL.
Published by Mad Libs, an imprint of Penguin Random House LLC.

MAD LIBS® is fun to play with friends, but you can also play it by yourself! To begin with, DO NOT look at the story on the page below. Fill in the blanks on this page with the words called for. Then, using the words you have selected, fill in the blank spaces in the story.

Now you've created your own hilarious MAD LIBS® game!

WITH GREAT POWER...

ADJECTIVE _____

PERSON IN ROOM _____

PLURAL NOUN _____

NUMBER _____

NOUN _____

VERB ENDING IN "ING" _____

ADJECTIVE _____

VERB ENDING IN "ING" _____

PLURAL NOUN _____

PART OF THE BODY _____

PART OF THE BODY (PLURAL) _____

NOUN _____

PLURAL NOUN _____

MAD LIBS

WITH GREAT POWER...

Spider-Man has a/an _____ array of spider powers to help
ADJECTIVE

him fight crime and make the streets safe for people like _____.
PERSON IN ROOM

He uses his **super strength** to lift heavy _____ up to
PLURAL NOUN

_____ tons. He can toss a/an _____ like it's nothing at
NUMBER   NOUN

all. He's also invulnerable. When a bad guy is _____
VERB ENDING IN "ING"

nearby, Spidey's **spider-sense** goes nuts. It warns him about

_____ danger and possible harm. All that jumping and
ADJECTIVE

_____ that Spidey does is because he's got **enhanced**
VERB ENDING IN "ING"

reflexes and agility. He can dodge _____ and hop from
PLURAL NOUN

place to place in the blink of a/an _____. Spider-Man may be
PART OF THE BODY

best known for his **wall-crawling** skills. His _____
PART OF THE BODY (PLURAL)

stick to any surface. Don't forget Spidey is also a **genius**! He invented

his _____ Shooters and Spider _____.
NOUN   PLURAL NOUN

MAD LIBS® is fun to play with friends, but you can also play it by yourself! To begin with, DO NOT look at the story on the page below. Fill in the blanks on this page with the words called for. Then, using the words you have selected, fill in the blank spaces in the story.

Now you've created your own hilarious MAD LIBS® game!

SPIDER-MAN VERSUS DOCTOR OCTOPUS

VERB _____

ADJECTIVE _____

NOUN _____

PART OF THE BODY (PLURAL) _____

VERB ENDING IN "ING" _____

ANIMAL _____

VERB _____

NOUN _____

SILLY WORD _____

NOUN _____

OCCUPATION _____

NOUN _____

CELEBRITY _____

PLURAL NOUN _____

TYPE OF LIQUID _____

VERB ENDING IN "ING" _____

MAD☺LIBS®
SPIDER-MAN VERSUS
DOCTOR OCTOPUS

Spider-Man: Hey, Doc Ock! Sorry to _____ so unexpectedly, but
VERB

I'm shutting you and your _____ experiments down for good.
ADJECTIVE

Doctor Octopus: How dare you enter my _____ , Spider-Man?!
NOUN

I am Dr. Otto Octavius, and my _____ will destroy
PART OF THE BODY (PLURAL)

you!

Spider-Man: Yikes. Calm down, dude. You're _____ a
VERB ENDING IN "ING"

little too hard. Be a good little _____ so I can _____
ANIMAL   VERB

you to jail.

Doctor Octopus: Get away before I squish you like a/an _____ .
NOUN

Spider-Man: _____! Okay, it's time to get serious,
SILLY WORD

_____ . After all, who do you think you are, the _____
NOUN   OCCUPATION

of England?

Doctor Octopus: You make too many jokes, Spider-Man. This isn't a

game of _____ -ball.
NOUN

Spider-Man: It isn't? I had no idea! I thought I was _____ .
CELEBRITY

Now grab your _____ , finish the last sip of your
PLURAL NOUN

_____ , and let's get _____ !
TYPE OF LIQUID   VERB ENDING IN "ING"

MAD LIBS® is fun to play with friends, but you can also play it by yourself! To begin with, DO NOT look at the story on the page below. Fill in the blanks on this page with the words called for. Then, using the words you have selected, fill in the blank spaces in the story.

Now you've created your own hilarious MAD LIBS® game!

HOW TO HAVE A SECRET IDENTITY

ADJECTIVE _____

VERB ENDING IN "ING" _____

NOUN _____

ADJECTIVE _____

NOUN _____

PART OF THE BODY _____

VERB _____

VERB ENDING IN "ING" _____

NOUN _____

PLURAL NOUN _____

PERSON IN ROOM _____

SILLY WORD _____

ADJECTIVE _____

NOUN _____

ADJECTIVE _____

ADJECTIVE _____

MAD LIBS®
HOW TO HAVE
A SECRET IDENTITY

Hey! It's me, your _____ neighborhood Spider-Man! You
                  ADJECTIVE

might be _____ yourself, "How does Spidey keep his
       VERB ENDING IN "ING"

_____ a secret?" That's a/an _____ question. You're
  NOUN   ADJECTIVE

so smart to ask. Well, first and foremost, I wear a/an _____.
                                               NOUN

That way no one can see my _____. Don't I look good? The
                      PART OF THE BODY

ladies sure seem to think so. I also like to _____ fast so no one
                                VERB

can see me _____! That's why they call me the great
         VERB ENDING IN "ING"

_____! Just kidding. No one calls me that. Oh, and I make
  NOUN

sure not to tell too many _____ that I'm a super hero.
                  PLURAL NOUN

Maybe just _____ and my teddy bear, _____.
        PERSON IN ROOM   SILLY WORD

Speaking from experience, the most _____ advice I can give is
                         ADJECTIVE

to make sure your _____ doesn't find your _____
            NOUN   ADJECTIVE

costume lying around. If that happens it could blow your

_____ identity sky high. Trust me—you don't want that
  ADJECTIVE

happening!

MAD LIBS® is fun to play with friends, but you can also play it by yourself! To begin with, DO NOT look at the story on the page below. Fill in the blanks on this page with the words called for. Then, using the words you have selected, fill in the blank spaces in the story.

Now you've created your own hilarious MAD LIBS® game!

TORMENT OF THE LIZARD

VERB ENDING IN "ING" _____

ADJECTIVE _____

EXCLAMATION _____

OCCUPATION _____

ADJECTIVE _____

PART OF THE BODY _____

PLURAL NOUN _____

ADJECTIVE _____

COLOR _____

PLURAL NOUN _____

ANIMAL _____

ADJECTIVE _____

ADJECTIVE _____

VERB (PAST TENSE) _____

OCCUPATION _____

MAD LIBS®

TORMENT OF THE LIZARD

Peter's spider-sense began _____ as he heard a/an

VERB ENDING IN "ING"

_____ _____ from inside the laboratory of

ADJECTIVE · EXCLAMATION

Dr. Curt Connors. He rushed in to find his favorite _____

OCCUPATION

on the floor. "Dr. Connors, are you _____?" asked Peter.

ADJECTIVE

Connors had lost his _____ in an explosion not too long ago.

PART OF THE BODY

Now he was studying _____ and searching for a way to

PLURAL NOUN

grow his _____ arm back. "Leave me alone, Peter!" shouted

ADJECTIVE

Connors. His skin turned _____ and small _____

COLOR · PLURAL NOUN

began growing all over his body. He was turning into a/an

_____! "Whoa!" exclaimed Peter. "Those are some

ANIMAL

_____ teeth you've got there." Connors let out a/an

ADJECTIVE

_____ growl. He snarled at Peter and _____

ADJECTIVE · VERB (PAST TENSE)

out the window in fear. He was no longer an ordinary _____;

OCCUPATION

he had become the fearsome Lizard.

MAD LIBS® is fun to play with friends, but you can also play it by yourself! To begin with, DO NOT look at the story on the page below. Fill in the blanks on this page with the words called for. Then, using the words you have selected, fill in the blank spaces in the story.

Now you've created your own hilarious MAD LIBS® game!

ATTACK OF THE GREEN GOBLIN

VERB _____

VERB ENDING IN "ING" _____

A PLACE _____

VERB _____

TYPE OF FOOD _____

NOUN _____

SILLY WORD _____

ADJECTIVE _____

OCCUPATION _____

COLOR _____

NOUN _____

COLOR _____

A PLACE _____

ADJECTIVE _____

PLURAL NOUN _____

EXCLAMATION _____

ADJECTIVE _____

NOUN _____

MAD LIBS®
ATTACK OF THE GREEN GOBLIN

Green Goblin: Hahahaha! _____ me if you dare, Spider-Man!
VERB

Spider-Man: Oh, don't worry, Goblin. If there's one thing I do, it's

that! Now stop _____ so I can catch you and take you
VERB ENDING IN "ING"

to (the) _____.
A PLACE

Green Goblin: I'm going to _____ you like a piece of
VERB

_____, wall crawler. You'll be a/an _____ when I'm
TYPE OF FOOD   NOUN

through with you.

Spider-Man: Talk to me for real, _____. You're Norman
SILLY WORD

Osborn, _____ inventor and _____ of science. Why
ADJECTIVE   OCCUPATION

are you dressed up like some _____ _____ all of a sudden?
COLOR   NOUN

Green Goblin: Norman Osborn is no more! I am the _____
COLOR

Goblin now and forever. First I'll take over (the) _____, and
A PLACE

then I'll destroy you once and for all.

Spider-Man: Now you're just acting _____!
ADJECTIVE

Green Goblin: Enough talk! Try one of my Goblin _____!
PLURAL NOUN

Spider-Man: _____! All right, that's it! Now the _____
EXCLAMATION   ADJECTIVE

Spider-Man is going to teach you a/an _____ you'll never forget!
NOUN

MAD LIBS® is fun to play with friends, but you can also play it by yourself! To begin with, DO NOT look at the story on the page below. Fill in the blanks on this page with the words called for. Then, using the words you have selected, fill in the blank spaces in the story.

Now you've created your own hilarious MAD LIBS® game!

THE DEADLY FOES OF SPIDER-MAN

ADJECTIVE _____

VERB _____

PART OF THE BODY _____

OCCUPATION _____

NOUN _____

ADJECTIVE _____

PLURAL NOUN _____

PLURAL NOUN _____

NOUN _____

TYPE OF LIQUID _____

ADJECTIVE _____

PLURAL NOUN _____

NOUN _____

ANIMAL _____

ADJECTIVE _____

MAD LIBS®
THE DEADLY FOES OF SPIDER-MAN

When a group of Spidey's _____ bad guys get together, you
ADJECTIVE

know it's going to be trouble!

Shocker wears a pair of vibro-shock gauntlets that lets him _____
VERB

his enemies right in their _____. He's not a nice guy.
PART OF THE BODY

Beetle was a lowly _____ until he built an armored suit that
OCCUPATION

made him look like a metal _____, thus beginning his life of
NOUN

crime.

Boomerang uses his _____ skills to throw specialized
ADJECTIVE

_____ that he stores on the outside of his costume.
PLURAL NOUN

Hydro-Man gained his _____ when he was tossed into
PLURAL NOUN

a/an _____ and exposed to volcanic gases. Now he can turn
NOUN

his body into _____!
TYPE OF LIQUID

Speed Demon invented a/an _____ chemical formula that gives
ADJECTIVE

him super speed. Now he uses his _____ to commit crimes.
PLURAL NOUN

Rhino is an enormous _____ whose suit of armor gives him
NOUN

the strength of a/an _____. He's got a/an _____
ANIMAL ADJECTIVE

attitude to boot.

From MARVEL'S SPIDER-MAN MAD LIBS® • Copyright © 2017 MARVEL.
Published by Mad Libs, an imprint of Penguin Random House LLC.

MAD LIBS® is fun to play with friends, but you can also play it by yourself! To begin with, DO NOT look at the story on the page below. Fill in the blanks on this page with the words called for. Then, using the words you have selected, fill in the blank spaces in the story.

Now you've created your own hilarious MAD LIBS® game!

FRIENDLY NEIGHBORHOOD SPIDER-MAN

EXCLAMATION _____

VERB ENDING IN "ING" _____

ADJECTIVE _____

PART OF THE BODY (PLURAL) _____

VERB _____

TYPE OF LIQUID _____

TYPE OF FOOD _____

NOUN _____

VERB _____

ANIMAL _____

A PLACE _____

NUMBER _____

PLURAL NOUN _____

A PLACE _____

ADJECTIVE _____

COLOR _____

MAD⊚LIBS®
FRIENDLY NEIGHBORHOOD
SPIDER-MAN

Dear Kingpin,

_____! I just finished _____ your
   EXCLAMATION   VERB ENDING IN "ING"

_____ group of ninjas right in their _____.
  ADJECTIVE   PART OF THE BODY (PLURAL)

It was super fun. Did you know that ninjas _____ when they
                                                 VERB

get smacked? I didn't. They don't teach you that in hero school. You're

probably at home drinking _____ and eating
                                TYPE OF LIQUID

_____ right now, so I'll keep this brief. I'm taking you and
 TYPE OF FOOD

your crime _____ down, buddy. _____ up because
          NOUN   VERB

the spectacular Spider-Man is doing whatever a/an _____ can
                                          ANIMAL

to clean up (the) _____ and kick you to the curb. I'm serious.
                  A PLACE

Grab your _____ _____ and go to (the)
           NUMBER   PLURAL NOUN

_____. And take all your stinking ninjas with you! Honestly,
 A PLACE

those guys think they're so _____ in their _____
                          ADJECTIVE   COLOR

suits, but they're super gross.

Love you! (You're going down.)

Your Friendly Neighborhood Spider-Man

MAD LIBS® is fun to play with friends, but you can also play it by yourself! To begin with, DO NOT look at the story on the page below. Fill in the blanks on this page with the words called for. Then, using the words you have selected, fill in the blank spaces in the story.

Now you've created your own hilarious MAD LIBS® game!

THE DAILY BUGLE

NOUN _____

ADJECTIVE _____

PLURAL NOUN _____

PART OF THE BODY _____

COLOR _____

TYPE OF FOOD _____

VERB _____

ADVERB _____

PLURAL NOUN _____

PLURAL NOUN _____

TYPE OF FOOD _____

NUMBER _____

PLURAL NOUN _____

ADJECTIVE _____

PLURAL NOUN _____

NOUN _____

VERB _____

OCCUPATION _____

MAD LIBS®

THE DAILY BUGLE

Peter Parker,

I received your photographs of that so-called hero, Spider-Man. While

I wish we could banish that _____ from this _____
_____NOUN_____ADJECTIVE

city forever, your _____ aren't all bad. You've got a good
_____PLURAL NOUN

_____. But the photos were too _____ and it looked
PART OF THE BODY_____COLOR

like one of them had _____ on it. That's a problem. At the
_____TYPE OF FOOD

Daily Bugle I _____ quality. I _____ consider the
_____VERB_____ADVERB

_____ that I share with my readers. If you want to work
___PLURAL NOUN

here, you've got to get even better. Study your _____, eat
_____PLURAL NOUN

your _____, and call me when you turn _____. Then
___TYPE OF FOOD_____NUMBER

I'll see about putting your _____ in my _____
_____PLURAL NOUN_____ADJECTIVE

news source. Until then, don't send me any more Spider-Man

_____. He's a menace to this _____ and I
___PLURAL NOUN_____NOUN

_____ him!
____VERB

Sincerely,

J. Jonah Jameson, _____ in Chief
_____OCCUPATION

MAD LIBS® is fun to play with friends, but you can also play it by yourself! To begin with, DO NOT look at the story on the page below. Fill in the blanks on this page with the words called for. Then, using the words you have selected, fill in the blank spaces in the story.

Now you've created your own hilarious MAD LIBS® game!

NIGHT OF THE BLACK CAT

ADVERB _____

A PLACE _____

NUMBER _____

NOUN _____

ADJECTIVE _____

OCCUPATION _____

VERB ENDING IN "ING" _____

COLOR _____

ANIMAL _____

VERB ENDING IN "ING" _____

VERB _____

NOUN _____

A PLACE _____

PLURAL NOUN _____

NOUN _____

NOUN _____

VERB ENDING IN "ING" _____

MAD LIBS®

NIGHT OF THE BLACK CAT

Spider-Man _____ stepped into (the) _____ and
                 ADVERB   A PLACE

noticed the vault door was open. He scanned the room to see

_____ crooks tied up in a corner. "Someone did my job already!"
NUMBER

said Spider-Man as his _____ echoed in the _____
                            NOUN   ADJECTIVE

bank. "But I'm the only _____ around here." "Not anymore,"
                            OCCUPATION

said the Black Cat, _____ down from above. "Who
                     VERB ENDING IN "ING"

are you?" asked Spider-Man. "My name is the _____
                                                    COLOR

_____. I caught these men _____ and was
   ANIMAL   VERB ENDING IN "ING"

able to _____ them before they got away." Spider-Man was
          VERB

surprised by this new hero, but was she a/an _____? He had
                                                    NOUN

a few questions. "What were you doing in (the) _____ in the
                                                  A PLACE

first place? The _____ were locked," Spider-Man said. The
                  PLURAL NOUN

Black Cat pulled a/an _____ out of her pocket and smiled.
                           NOUN

"Well, _____, that's a mystery for another time," she said,
          NOUN

_____ out the window into the night.
VERB ENDING IN "ING"

MAD LIBS® is fun to play with friends, but you can also play it by yourself! To begin with, DO NOT look at the story on the page below. Fill in the blanks on this page with the words called for. Then, using the words you have selected, fill in the blank spaces in the story.

Now you've created your own hilarious MAD LIBS® game!

SPIDEY-SENSES

NOUN _____

PLURAL NOUN _____

COLOR _____

ADJECTIVE _____

TYPE OF FOOD _____

FIRST NAME (MALE) _____

ADJECTIVE _____

NOUN _____

PLURAL NOUN _____

VEHICLE _____

VERB _____

NOUN _____

MAD LIBS

SPIDEY-SENSES

How well do you know your Web Slinger? Take this quiz and see!

1. What is the name of the famous storyline where the _____
NOUN

created a bunch of _____ of Spider-Man?
PLURAL NOUN

(A) Spider-Man vs. the Scorpion (B) Maximum Carnage

(C) The Clone Saga (D) Assault of the Rhino

2. Spidey's _____ costume was a/an _____ alien
COLOR   ADJECTIVE

that wanted to eat people like they were _____.
TYPE OF FOOD

What was its name?

(A) Silvermane (B) Black Tarantula (C) The Purple People Eater

(D) Venom

3. Before Peter's Uncle _____ passed away, he gave him
FIRST NAME (MALE)

a/an _____ piece of _____. With great _____
ADJECTIVE   NOUN   PLURAL NOUN

comes . . . what? (A) immense potential (B) great responsibility

(C) awesome cars (D) danger and uncertainty

4. Spider-Man once had a/an _____ that could _____
VEHICLE   VERB

up a/an _____! What did he call it? (A) The Spider-Mobile
NOUN

(B) The Wall Crawler (C) The Stinger (D) Edna

MAD LIBS® is fun to play with friends, but you can also play it by yourself! To begin with, DO NOT look at the story on the page below. Fill in the blanks on this page with the words called for. Then, using the words you have selected, fill in the blank spaces in the story.

Now you've created your own hilarious MAD LIBS® game!

PEP TALK

VERB _____

TYPE OF FOOD _____

ADJECTIVE _____

VERB _____

ADJECTIVE _____

PART OF THE BODY _____

PERSON IN ROOM _____

VERB _____

NOUN _____

A PLACE _____

NOUN _____

VERB ENDING IN "ING" _____

PLURAL NOUN _____

CELEBRITY _____

EXCLAMATION _____

MAD LIBS®

PEP TALK

Aunt May: Peter, I need to _____ with you.
VERB

Peter: What's up, Aunt May? Did you make _____ again?
TYPE OF FOOD

I'm always game for a/an _____ treat.
ADJECTIVE

Aunt May: No, Peter. I want to _____ about something else.
VERB

You've been very _____ lately. Is everything okay?
ADJECTIVE

Peter: Yeah! Though my _____ is tingling like crazy.
PART OF THE BODY

Crash!

Aunt May: Did you hear that? Something must be going on at

_____'s house.
PERSON IN ROOM

Peter: Um, I have to _____! I just remembered I have to
VERB

pick up a/an _____ at (the) _____. It's for my
NOUN A PLACE

_____ project.
NOUN

Aunt May: But we're not done _____, Peter.
VERB ENDING IN "ING"

Peter: Sorry, Aunt May! You know how it is with me and

_____. I'm like their _____. I promise to be
PLURAL NOUN CELEBRITY

back before you can say "_____!"
EXCLAMATION

MAD LIBS® is fun to play with friends, but you can also play it by yourself! To begin with, DO NOT look at the story on the page below. Fill in the blanks on this page with the words called for. Then, using the words you have selected, fill in the blank spaces in the story.

Now you've created your own hilarious MAD LIBS® game!

HEROES OF THE SPIDER-VERSE

ADJECTIVE _____

ADJECTIVE _____

NOUN _____

NOUN _____

VERB _____

PERSON IN ROOM _____

SILLY WORD _____

NOUN _____

VERB ENDING IN "ING" _____

ADJECTIVE _____

NUMBER _____

PERSON IN ROOM _____

VERB _____

PLURAL NOUN _____

ADJECTIVE _____

NOUN _____

MAD LIBS
HEROES OF THE
SPIDER-VERSE

When things get _____, Spidey calls on other _____
                    ADJECTIVE   ADJECTIVE

heroes from across time and space to help him out! **Miles Morales** was

bitten by a genetically enhanced _____. He gained super
                                        NOUN

strength, _____ blasts, and the ability to _____
              NOUN   VERB

himself. Inspired by the heroism of _____, he became the
                                        PERSON IN ROOM

ultimate SPIDER-MAN. In an alternate future, **May** "_____"
                                                        SILLY WORD

Parker is the _____ of Peter Parker and Mary Jane Watson.
                      NOUN

May developed the same powers as her father and began

_____ criminals as SPIDER-GIRL. **Ben Reilly** is a
VERB ENDING IN "ING"

clone of Peter Parker created by the _____ Jackal. For
                                            ADJECTIVE

_____ years, he believed he was _____. After learning
    NUMBER   PERSON IN ROOM

the truth, he decided to _____ crime as the SCARLET
                              VERB

SPIDER. In the future, **Miguel O'Hara** studied _____ at
                                                      PLURAL NOUN

Alchemax. A/An _____ serum altered his _____,
                    ADJECTIVE   NOUN

giving him the abilities of a spider. Miguel donned a costume to become

SPIDER-MAN 2099.

MAD LIBS® is fun to play with friends, but you can also play it by yourself! To begin with, DO NOT look at the story on the page below. Fill in the blanks on this page with the words called for. Then, using the words you have selected, fill in the blank spaces in the story.

Now you've created your own hilarious MAD LIBS® game!

DEAR MARY JANE...

NOUN _____

ADJECTIVE _____

VERB ENDING IN "ING" _____

TYPE OF LIQUID _____

NOUN _____

ADJECTIVE _____

ADJECTIVE _____

PLURAL NOUN _____

COLOR _____

SILLY WORD _____

OCCUPATION _____

VERB _____

A PLACE _____

TYPE OF LIQUID _____

TYPE OF FOOD _____

VERB _____

A PLACE _____

NUMBER _____

MAD LIBS®

DEAR MARY JANE...

Hey MJ,

How are you? I hope getting this _____ from me isn't
                                        NOUN

_____ . I've been _____ to give it to you for
  ADJECTIVE   VERB ENDING IN "ING"

a while now. I want to apologize for what happened. I didn't mean to

spill _____ all over your _____ project. It was
      TYPE OF LIQUID   NOUN

a/an _____ accident. I guess I was just nervous because I like
      ADJECTIVE

you. Not in a/an _____ way, more in the way I like
                  ADJECTIVE

_____ . I just think you're cool. It's probably because of
  PLURAL NOUN

your _____ hair and the way you call me _____ .
      COLOR   SILLY WORD

Oh, and I like that you want to be a/an _____ someday. It's
                                          OCCUPATION

awesome. Let's _____ sometime. We can go to (the)
                  VERB

_____ , have a/an _____ and maybe a slice of
  A PLACE   TYPE OF LIQUID

_____ . _____ me back and let me know. I'll be in
  TYPE OF FOOD   VERB

(the) _____ , Room _____ .
        A PLACE   NUMBER

Peter

MAD LIBS® is fun to play with friends, but you can also play it by yourself! To begin with, DO NOT look at the story on the page below. Fill in the blanks on this page with the words called for. Then, using the words you have selected, fill in the blank spaces in the story.

Now you've created your own hilarious MAD LIBS® game!

ARE YOU A WEB HEAD?

ADJECTIVE _____

SILLY WORD _____

VERB _____

PLURAL NOUN _____

NOUN _____

CELEBRITY _____

VERB _____

A PLACE _____

SILLY WORD _____

EXCLAMATION _____

PART OF THE BODY _____

ADJECTIVE _____

VERB _____

ADJECTIVE _____

PLURAL NOUN _____

ADJECTIVE _____

MAD LIBS

ARE YOU A WEB HEAD?

It's your pal, Spider-Man. I'm back to talk about my nicknames. I have

a lot of them. Most are pretty _____, but every so often,
                              ADJECTIVE

someone will call me a/an _____. It makes me _____.
                          SILLY WORD   VERB

My close _____ call me Spidey or _____. Hey,
          PLURAL NOUN   NOUN

don't laugh! Someday _____ might play me in a movie. You
                      CELEBRITY

wouldn't _____ at them, would you? I didn't think so. In (the)
          VERB

_____ they call me _____. Fancy, huh? I think that
 A PLACE   SILLY WORD

translates to Web Head. Or was that Web Slinger? _____!
                                                  EXCLAMATION

I think it was Wall Crawler, actually. Trying to remember makes my

_____ hurt. When a bad guy tries to call me a/an
 PART OF THE BODY

_____ name I tell them, "Don't _____ with the
 ADJECTIVE   VERB

_____ Arachnid!" Those _____ can be so rude.
 ADJECTIVE   PLURAL NOUN

But I think I like _____ Neighborhood Spider-Man the most.
                    ADJECTIVE

Nothing beats a classic!

From MARVEL'S SPIDER-MAN MAD LIBS® • Copyright © 2017 MARVEL.
Published by Mad Libs, an imprint of Penguin Random House LLC.

MAD LIBS® is fun to play with friends, but you can also play it by yourself! To begin with, DO NOT look at the story on the page below. Fill in the blanks on this page with the words called for. Then, using the words you have selected, fill in the blank spaces in the story.

Now you've created your own hilarious MAD LIBS® game!

THE SINISTER SIX STRIKE

ADJECTIVE _____

ADJECTIVE _____

ADJECTIVE _____

NOUN _____

VERB (PAST TENSE) _____

COLOR _____

ADJECTIVE _____

ANIMAL (PLURAL) _____

ADJECTIVE _____

NOUN _____

VERB (PAST TENSE) _____

VERB ENDING IN "ING" _____

PART OF THE BODY (PLURAL) _____

ANIMAL _____

NOUN _____

EXCLAMATION _____

ADVERB _____

MAD LIBS®

THE SINISTER SIX STRIKE

"Hi, guys. You look pretty _____. How can I help turn those
                         ADJECTIVE
frowns upside down?" asked Spider-Man. The Sinister Six had Spidey

cornered. There was no way out and things looked pretty

_____. First, Sandman blasted Spider-Man with a/an
   ADJECTIVE

_____ _____. Then it was Electro's turn. He
   ADJECTIVE   NOUN

_____ the web slinger with _____ lightning.
VERB (PAST TENSE)   COLOR

Then Mysterio created a/an _____ illusion. He made Spider-
                                ADJECTIVE

Man see a bunch of cute _____. While Spidey was
                          ANIMAL (PLURAL)

distracted, Kraven used his _____ strength to toss him like
                              ADJECTIVE

a/an _____. Finally, Vulture _____ from
       NOUN   VERB (PAST TENSE)

above, picking up Spidey and _____ him right at the
                                VERB ENDING IN "ING"

_____ of Doctor Octopus. The evil Doctor used his
PART OF THE BODY (PLURAL)

_____ _____ to pull Spidey up from the ground.
   ANIMAL   NOUN

"_____, Ock!" Spider-Man said _____. "Can
   EXCLAMATION   ADVERB

you call a nice doctor? I'm kind of woozy."

MAD LIBS® is fun to play with friends, but you can also play it by yourself! To begin with, DO NOT look at the story on the page below. Fill in the blanks on this page with the words called for. Then, using the words you have selected, fill in the blank spaces in the story.

Now you've created your own hilarious MAD LIBS® game!

SPIDER-WOMAN: AN AMAZING FRIEND

A PLACE _____

NOUN _____

FOREIGN COUNTRY _____

ADJECTIVE _____

NOUN _____

SILLY WORD _____

VERB _____

VERB _____

ADJECTIVE _____

ADJECTIVE _____

PART OF THE BODY _____

VERB _____

ADJECTIVE _____

NOUN _____

EXCLAMATION _____

VERB _____

VERB _____

MAD LIBS
SPIDER-WOMAN:
AN AMAZING FRIEND

Spider-Man: Well, well, well. Look who it is! Jessica Drew,

SPIDER-WOMAN. What are you doing here in (the)_____?

  A PLACE

Spider-Woman: I'm tracking down some super villains. They stole

the _____ of _____. It's up to me to get it back.

  NOUN   FOREIGN COUNTRY

Spider-Man: Wow. That's _____. I was going to go play

  ADJECTIVE

_____-ball today, but now I guess I'll help you instead.

  NOUN

Spider-Woman: That's okay, _____. Thanks for the offer,

  SILLY WORD

but I can _____ this by myself.

  VERB

Spider-Man: Will you _____ those bad guys with a/an

  VERB

_____ venom blast? That would be cool.

  ADJECTIVE

Spider-Woman: Maybe. But a/an _____ jab to the

  ADJECTIVE

_____ might take them out quicker.

PART OF THE BODY

Spider-Man: I didn't know you could _____ like that.

  VERB

Spider-Woman: Don't you remember? I'm also a/an _____

  ADJECTIVE

_____ for S.H.I.E.L.D.

  NOUN

Spider-Man: _____! Is there anything you can't _____?

  EXCLAMATION   VERB

Spider-Woman: I wish I could make you _____ less.

  VERB

MAD LIBS® is fun to play with friends, but you can also play it by yourself! To begin with, DO NOT look at the story on the page below. Fill in the blanks on this page with the words called for. Then, using the words you have selected, fill in the blank spaces in the story.

Now you've created your own hilarious MAD LIBS® game!

ARACHNID ALLIES

VERB ENDING IN "ING" _____

A PLACE _____

PLURAL NOUN _____

ADJECTIVE _____

PLURAL NOUN _____

ADJECTIVE _____

VERB _____

NOUN _____

PLURAL NOUN _____

ADJECTIVE _____

ADJECTIVE _____

ADJECTIVE _____

NOUN _____

ADJECTIVE _____

ARTICLE OF CLOTHING _____

MAD LIBS®

ARACHNID ALLIES

When Spider-Man isn't _____ around (the)

_____, he's hanging out with his _____ in Queens.
VERB ENDING IN "ING"

A PLACE   PLURAL NOUN

Gwen Stacy is a/an _____ young lady who knows her
                                    ADJECTIVE

_____. It's no wonder Peter has such a/an _____
PLURAL NOUN   ADJECTIVE

crush on her.

Flash Thompson likes to _____ Peter around a lot like a
                                        VERB

bully. He'd rather play _____-ball than study. Go figure.
                              NOUN

Mary Jane Watson is one of Peter's best _____. She's
                                                    PLURAL NOUN

always there for him, even when things are _____. Peter also
                                                    ADJECTIVE

thinks she's _____.
                ADJECTIVE

Harry Osborn and Peter have a/an _____ friendship. Peter
                                            ADJECTIVE

would do anything to help him, even though Harry's _____ is
                                                            NOUN

actually the Green Goblin.

Dear _____ **Aunt May** has no idea Peter is really Spider-Man.
        ADJECTIVE

If he leaves his _____ out for her to wash, he'll be in
                    ARTICLE OF CLOTHING

big trouble.

From MARVEL'S SPIDER-MAN MAD LIBS® • Copyright © 2017 MARVEL.
Published by Mad Libs, an imprint of Penguin Random House LLC.

MAD LIBS® is fun to play with friends, but you can also play it by yourself! To begin with, DO NOT look at the story on the page below. Fill in the blanks on this page with the words called for. Then, using the words you have selected, fill in the blank spaces in the story.

Now you've created your own hilarious MAD LIBS® game!

NO MORE WALL CRAWLERS, BY J. JONAH JAMESON

CITY _____

ADJECTIVE _____

NOUN _____

OCCUPATION _____

ADJECTIVE _____

VERB _____

EXCLAMATION _____

NOUN _____

ADJECTIVE _____

VERB _____

ANIMAL _____

NOUN _____

SILLY WORD _____

COLOR _____

NOUN _____

NOUN _____

MAD LIBS®
NO MORE WALL CRAWLERS,
BY J. JONAH JAMESON

I love _____. I think it's the most _____ place on the
        CITY   ADJECTIVE

planet. That's why I believe we need to get rid of Spider-Man. That

_____ thinks he's the _____ of New York. Except
     NOUN   OCCUPATION

Spider-Man really attracts _____ villains who _____
                       ADJECTIVE   VERB

the city because of him. _____! I think I speak for the
                           EXCLAMATION

people when I say I'm sick of it! That _____ needs to be
                                     NOUN

stopped! Some people think he's a/an _____ hero, but not me.
                                 ADJECTIVE

Sure, he might _____ people sometimes or save a/an
                   VERB

_____ caught in a/an _____ every now and again.
     ANIMAL   NOUN

But so what? Big _____! Spider-Man is nothing but a/an
                   SILLY WORD

_____ _____ and we have to get rid of him! If you
    COLOR   NOUN

see him on the street, throw a/an _____ at him and say it's
                              NOUN

from me, J. Jonah Jameson!

MAD LIBS® is fun to play with friends, but you can also play it by yourself! To begin with, DO NOT look at the story on the page below. Fill in the blanks on this page with the words called for. Then, using the words you have selected, fill in the blank spaces in the story.

Now you've created your own hilarious MAD LIBS® game!

BODY SWITCH

PART OF THE BODY _____

PART OF THE BODY _____

PLURAL NOUN _____

PLURAL NOUN _____

NUMBER _____

PLURAL NOUN _____

ANIMAL (PLURAL) _____

VERB _____

SILLY WORD _____

NOUN _____

TYPE OF FOOD _____

ADJECTIVE _____

NOUN _____

PART OF THE BODY _____

NOUN _____

MAD LIBS®
BODY SWITCH

Spider-Man looked into the mirror. But it wasn't *his* _____
PART OF THE BODY

that stared back. "I look like Doc Ock!" Spidey shouted. "My

_____ is gross, and I've got _____. What's going
PART OF THE BODY   PLURAL NOUN

on?!" Turns out Doctor Octopus had switched _____ with
PLURAL NOUN

Spider-Man. "At last I've done it!" Doc Ock shouted. "For _____
NUMBER

years I've planned for this moment. I studied _____ in
PLURAL NOUN

school. I tested the transfer process on _____. Now I
ANIMAL (PLURAL)

will _____, and there's nothing you can do about it!"
VERB

"Look here, _____! I want my _____ back right
SILLY WORD   NOUN

now!" Spider-Man shouted. "I feel like a/an _____." "With
TYPE OF FOOD

my incredible intellect and your _____ body, I will become
ADJECTIVE

the greatest _____ of all time," Doctor Octopus said, flexing
NOUN

his _____. "Not just an *AMAZING* Spider-Man but a
PART OF THE BODY

SUPERIOR one!" "I think I need a/an _____," Spidey sighed.
NOUN

Download Mad Libs today!

Join the millions of Mad Libs fans creating wacky and wonderful stories on our apps!